# FASCINATING FACTS
## for the
# WHOLE FAMILY

by

*Nayden Kostov*

# FASCINATING FACTS
## for the
# WHOLE FAMILY

by

*Nayden Kostov*

Luxembourg
2017

# FASCINATING FACTS FOR THE WHOLE FAMILY

| | |
|---|---|
| *Author:* | Nayden Kostov |
| *Illustrations:* | Pavel Kostov |
| *Editors:* | Jonathon Tabet and Andrea Leitenberger |

*Format:* 5,25 x 8

ISBN-13: 978-99959-980-5-9
ISBN-10: 999599805X

# CONTENTS

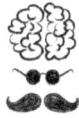

*By Nayden Kostov*

# PROLOGUE

Following the success of my website www.RaiseYourBrain. com and my books '1123 Hard to Believe Facts' and 'Which Is NOT True? - The Quiz Book' I decided to create my first trivia book for children. My aim was to entice them into reading and learning new stuff while having fun.

The book is dedicated to topics that kids adore: animals and human body. The lack of explicit sexuality, foul language or gore makes it a good read for anyone in the age range from 8 to 18 years (and their parents too ;) ).

A life hack if your child is NOT an avid reader: when you are preparing his/her lunch box, slip inside a couple of those facts. You could print out three facts every day to create some lunchtime fun for your kids and provoke their intellectual curiosity.

My son Pavel is 8 years old and really loves learning new things every day.

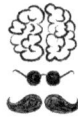

He helped me to handpick and order the facts. He also proudly did the illustrations.

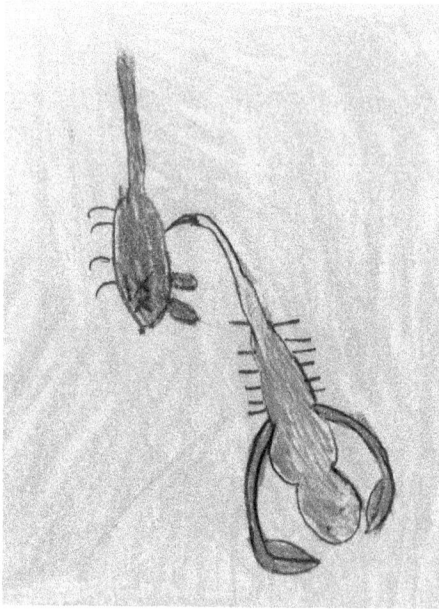

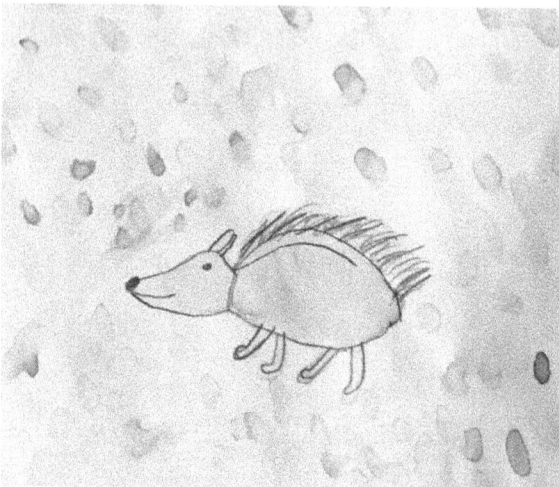

By Nayden Kostov

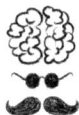

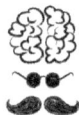

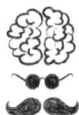

# AMAZING FACTS ABOUT CUTE ANIMALS

## Cats

1.   There are around 50 cat breeds. The most popular breed with a pedigree is the Persian cat.

2.   The smallest and largest pedigreed cats are the Singapura and the Maine Coon respectively.

3.   The word 'tabby' is believed to come from Attabiyah, a neighbourhood in Baghdad, Iraq.

4.   Cats (the Turkish Van being a notable exception) generally hate water and rain as their wet fur does not insulate well enough.

5.   Cats have twelve whiskers on each side of their face. Damaged whiskers significantly worsen their orientation skills.

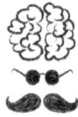

6.   Siamese cats in the Dutch embassy in Moscow, Russia, discovered microphones hidden by Soviet spies.

7.   Isaac Newton invented the cat flap.

8.   Cats cannot chew big chunks of food as their jaws do not move sideways.

9.   The cheetah is the only running cat; all others are leaping cats.

10.  Cats have 32 muscles to control their outer ear (humans have six).

11.  The heaviest cat ever weighed over 21 kg (46 pounds).

12.  The oldest cat ever lived 38 years.

13.  In 1871, the first cat show was held in London, UK.

14.  The oldest cat video available on YouTube was filmed in 1894.

15.  A cat has 230 bones but no collarbone, so it can pass through any opening larger than the size of its head.

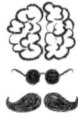

16. A cat's nose pad is unique, much alike human fingerprint.

17. Aspirin is extremely toxic for cats.

18. A cat's heart beats much faster than human one.

19. Cats sweat solely through their foot pads.

20. Cats spend two thirds of their life sleeping.

21. Cats clean their fur for about a third of their waking hours. They lick themselves mostly to remove human scents acquired through interaction with their owners.

22. Cats can predict earthquakes.

23. Cats sometimes are able to detect human cancer.

24. A cat's claws make climbing a tree piece of cake; however, getting down is much harder.

25. The claws on a cat's back paws do not retract and they are less sharp than the front ones.

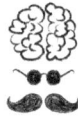

26. Cats cannot taste sweetness.

27. Adult cats only meow to communicate with humans.

28. Cats could survive a fall from the 15th floor of a building. Falling from lower heights (between 3rd and 7th floor) is in fact more dangerous for them as they do not have enough time to position their body correctly.

29. Cats rub against people to mark out territory with scent glands located on their head.

30. In ancient Egypt, family members would shave their eyebrows to mourn over a dead cat.

31. Smuggling a cat out of ancient Egypt was punishable by death.

32. The word for cat in ancient Egypt was 'mau'.

33. The Egyptian Mau is considered to be the oldest breed of cat.

34. The Egyptian goddess Bast had a woman's body and a cat's head.

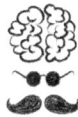

35. The largest known litter ever was 19 kittens large.

36. Cat owners are more likely to hold a graduate degree than the rest of population.

37. Almost 90 percent of cats in the US are spayed or neutered.

38. The biggest wildcat is the Siberian Tiger, with length of over 3.7 m (12 feet) and weight up to 320 kg (700 pounds). The smallest wildcat is the Black-footed cat, measuring less than 50 cm (20 inches) and maximal weight 1.2 kg (2.6 pounds).

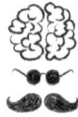

39. In 1997, a cat named Stubbs was elected honorary mayor of the town of Talkeetna, Alaska (USA).

40. The Islamic prophet Muhammad loved cats.

41. The 'black cat' superstition started in the 16th century. Black cats bring bad luck in many countries, but they are good luck in parts of the United Kingdom and Japan.

42. Cats can hear up to 80 kHz, allowing them to hear rodents' communications.

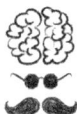

43. Despite their excellent night vision and far sight, cats have poorer close up vision than humans. They also have a blind spot in front of their nose.

44. Every year, millions of cats are eaten in Asia.

45. Female cats are mostly right-pawed, while male cats are more frequently left-pawed.

46. Cats can produce over 100 different sounds. Dogs make only about ten.

47. Humans and cats have similar regions in their brains that deal with emotions.

48. There are over 500 million domestic cats worldwide.

49. Historically, coats were also made of cat fur. It took on average 25 cat skins to make a single coat.

50. During the Spanish Inquisition, the widespread killing of cats (as they had been condemned by the Pope as a source of evil) resulted in rat population boom which in turn contributed to the spread of the plague.

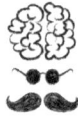

51. The first cat in space was a Parisian stray cat named Felicette.

52. A cat's maximum speed is 49 km/h (31 mph).

53. A cat can jump up to five times its own height.

54. A group of adult cats is called a clowder.

55. Kopi Luwak is a type of coffee prepared using coffee beans that have been eaten and partially digested by a civet cat.

56. The love for cats is called ailurophilia.

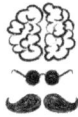

57.  Cats purr by using their larynx and diaphragm muscles. It is not yet understood however how their central nervous system controls these contractions.

58. Many Siamese cats are cross-eyed due to abnormal neurological connections between their eyes and brain.

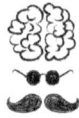

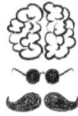

By Nayden Kostov

# Dogs

1. People domesticated dogs long ago, well before horses, donkeys, cattle, sheep, chickens, goats and cats.

2. Worldwide, there are more than 800 distinct dog breeds.

3. Homer is considered to be the first to mention a dog in writing.

4. A dog's wet nose helps it to collect more of the smelly chemicals in the air. They can smell termites, natural gas and dead bodies buried under dirt. Some dogs can smell cancerous tumours in human beings.

5. Young dogs have 28 milk teeth, later replaced by 42 permanent teeth.

6. Male dogs try to pee higher on a tree in order to leave a false impression that they are taller and more intimidating. The smells in a dog's urine give other dogs information about its gender, age, health and psychological condition.

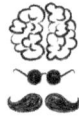

7.   Lampposts have fallen down due to the erosion caused by the corrosive chemicals in male dogs' urine.

8.   Dogs have the intellectual capacity of a 2.5-year-old child.

9.   One million US dogs are designated as the main beneficiary of their owner's last will and testament. In 1992, in Germany, a German Shepherd named Gunther IV inherited over 100 million US dollars.

10. A guy is more likely to get a girl's phone number if he walks a dog. The best choice is to walk a  Pit Bull.

11. Some insurance companies categorize the Akita breed as 'the world's worst dog'.

12. Worldwide, six million dog bites occur every year, with children being the most likely victims.

13. The Pekingese is a breed of dog, originating in China. It was bred to fit into the sleeves of the Chinese emperors' gowns.

14. Dogs detect sadness in their owners and often try to cheer them up by starting to cuddle them.

15. Dogs sometimes fake sickness to get attention.

16. On many occasions, dogs have warned people hours before an earthquake.

17. Dogs and elephants seem to be the only species to understand human gestures by instinct.

18. Dogs make circles before lying down because in the wild nature this would transform the long grass into a comfortable bed.

19. Anxious dogs wag their tails to the left and happy ones to the right (from their perspective).

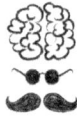

20. In 2014, a Tibetan Mastiff was sold in China for almost two million US dollars.

21. Dogs are capable of more than 100 facial expressions.

22. One in three dog owners talks to their pet on the phone.

23. Chained dogs tend to be 3 times more likely to bite than unchained ones. Female dogs bite twice as often as male dogs.

24. Dogs really cannot taste much of their food. Smell is what attracts dogs, not taste.

25. City dogs live two years more than country dogs.

26. The Canary Islands are named after a breed of dogs.

27. Dogs have 4 toes on their rear feet and 5 on their front ones.

28. A dog's pregnancy is typically less than 70 days.

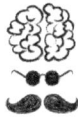

29. There are no hypoallergenic dogs.

30. Over 3,500 dogs served in the US Army during the Vietnam War.

31. The first dog tax was imposed in Germany in the 16<sup>th</sup> century.

31. The first dog tax was imposed in Germany in the 16th century.

32. A dog was hanged for witchcraft in Salem, Massachusetts (USA).

33. Basset Hounds have the longest ears. The one made famous by Hush Puppies was named Biggles.

34. Chewbacca from Star Wars saga was inspired by George Lucas's dog.

35. Dogs can be either left or right-pawed.

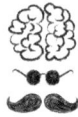

36. The Pharaoh Hound breed is the only breed of dogs that can 'blush'.

37. Dogs sweat mostly through their paw pads. They also dissipate heat by panting.

38. Dogs have a visual range of 255 degrees, whereas humans only have a field of vision of 182 degrees.

39. Dogs use up to 18 muscles to move each ear.

40. New-born puppies sleep 15 hours a day.

41. The phrase 'raining cats and dogs' emerged in Medieval England. After heavy downpours, the sewers would flood and the strays living within them would drown, their bodies rising to the street surface.

42. Ancient Egyptians revered dogs almost the same way they adored cats.

43. Many foods can threaten the health and life of a dog, for instance: grapes, coffee, chocolate, cooked onions, apple and pear seeds.

44. Dogs have a third eyelid.

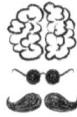

45. In the 13<sup>th</sup> century, the Mongol emperor Kublai Khan owned over 5,000 Mastiffs.

46. The dog in the Chinese zodiac symbolises loyalty.

47. Some cultures, such as the Hindu and Islamic cultures, do not really appreciate dogs. That may be due to the fact that rabies has always been endemic in the regions where these cultures were traditionally prevalent. For example, it is illegal to have a dog as a pet in Iran, unless it is used as a guard or hunting dog.

48. Laika, a Soviet stray dog, was the first mammal to go into orbit around the Earth.

49. Dalmatians are completely white at birth, and are often deaf.

50. The Basenji is the only barkless dog. But this breed can 'sing' when they are happy.

51. Dog could misread a human smile as an act of aggression, as dogs often try to intimidate each other through the showing of teeth.

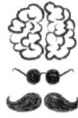

52. The origin of cutting a dog's tail may be tracked back to Roman times when people believed it prevented rabies.

53. In 1918, the German government started training guide dogs for war-blinded soldiers.

54. The average cost to train a certified search and rescue dog in the USA is around 10,000 dollars.

55. The biggest dog on record was an English Mastiff weighing 156 kg (343 pounds) and measuring 2.51 m (8 feet 3 inches) from nose to tail.

56. The smallest dog ever was a Yorkshire Terrier measuring 9 cm (3.5 inches) from nose to tail and weighting only 114 g (4 ounces).

57. Dogs hear sounds four times better than us whilst a dog's sense of smell is estimated to surpass a human's by a factor of 600,000.

58. The USA is the country with the highest pet dog count (more than 70,000,000). France comes second.

59. A dog's nose print is so unique that it can be used for identification.

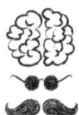

60. Two dogs are enough to form a pack.

61. Petting a dog can lower your blood pressure.

62. Only Chow Chow and Shar-pei dogs have blue tongues.

63. Dingos are not indigenous to Australia.

64. During the WW2, the Russians trained dogs for anti-tank suicide missions.

65. A dog's life expectancy is on average 16 years.

66. The oldest recorded age for a dog was almost 30 years.

67. The tallest dogs are the Great Dane and the Irish Wolfhound.

68. The Chihuahua is the smallest dog.

69. The St. Bernard is the heaviest dog breed.

70. Dogs are omnivorous and should not eat just meat.

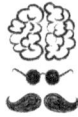

71. At birth puppies are blind, deaf and cannot smell. Puppies open their eyes at the age of 16 days and develop their sense of smell few days later.

72. Usually, the behaviour of a mongrel (mixed-breed dog) is most similar to the breed they most resemble visually.

73. All dogs, from the German Shepherd to the tiny Poodle, are direct descendants of wolves.

74. Dogs of any breed can mate, producing fertile offspring. Technically, they are all one species.

75. Dogs can regurgitate (vomit food) at will.

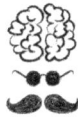

76. Barking Sands Beach in Hawaii, USA, is famous for its strange dry sand that 'barks like a dog'.

77. Two dogs survived the Titanic tragedy.

78. Confusingly, the Great Dane breed of dog comes from Germany rather than Denmark.

79. At the end of the Beatles' song 'A Day in the Life', Paul McCartney included an ultrasonic whistle to make his Shetland Sheepdog happy.

80. Prairie dogs are in fact rodents.

81. The Poodle's 'haircut' was used to improve their swimming abilities. The pom-poms' role is to keep their joints warm.

82. The Labrador Retriever is the most popular breed in the USA, Canada and the UK. Its original name was St. John's Newfoundland.

83. The Bloodhound breed were the first animal whose evidence was admissible in a US court of law. A Bloodhound breed's name comes from a time when it could only be owned by people of 'blood' or the upper class.

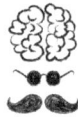

84. French poodles actually come from Germany (from German Pudel or Pudelhund, meaning 'splashing dog').

85. 'Greyhound' was mistakenly translated from Greishund, meaning 'ancient dog' in German. The breed name has nothing to do with the colour grey. They can run at over 70 km/h (46 mph).

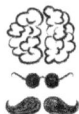

By Nayden Kostov

# Pandas

1.  The first live panda left China in 1936.

2.  The word 'panda' derives from the Nepalese 'poonya', meaning 'bamboo-eating animal'.

3.  The Chinese word for panda translates roughly as 'large bear cat'.

4.  Around 2,200 pandas are found in the wild. Another 200 are held in captivity. All captive pandas in the world are part of a breeding program.

5.  The giant panda is so close to extinction that it is referred to as a 'living fossil'.

6.  Male pandas have a bone inside their penis.

7.  The entire mating period takes only a few days every year. Five months after mating, a single cub is born in a bamboo nest.

8.  It is quite exceptional for a panda to give birth to twins in the wild. If it happens, the weaker cub of the twin pair does not normally survive. Pandas in captivity have twins more often.

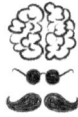

9.  Female pandas are single moms, raising their cubs on their own.

10. Many new-born pandas die from being accidentally crushed by their mothers.

11. At birth, cubs weigh 100 - 200 g (4 - 8 ounces) and measure 15 cm (6 inches).

12. A panda is blind for the first two months of its life and starts to crawl only at the age of three months.

13. Pandas are born all-white.

14. Mother panda holds the cub to her chest, just as humans do.

15. Pandas leave their parents at the age of 2 years.

16. Giant pandas have a special bone in their wrists called a 'pseudo-thumb'. The extra digit helps to grasp and tear the bamboo.

17. A panda's throat and guts are covered with a thick layer of mucus to protect against bamboo splinters.

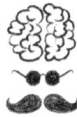

18. A carnivore-turned-veggie, panda subsists on bamboo. A panda eats around 20 kg (45 pounds) of bamboo shoots a day.

19. Pandas only eat 25 species of bamboo out of over 130 species available. Their strong jaws can crush bamboo shoots of up to 5 cm (2 inches) in thickness.

20. Pandas spend 12 hours a day eating bamboo. They also eat flowers, vines, green corn, rodents, fish and honey. In captivity pandas enjoy apples and carrots.

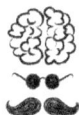

21. Bamboo dies off about every 20 years, forcing pandas to migrate to new pastures. Pandas can climb to an altitude of 4,000 m (13,000 feet) in search of food.

22. Unlike other bears, pandas do not hibernate. They simply cannot accumulate enough fat to afford to do so.

23. A panda has no permanent dwelling. Instead, it sleeps at the bottom of randomly selected trees.

24. DNA tests confirmed that giant pandas are indeed members of the bear family, and not relatives of racoons. The red panda, however, is a member of the raccoon family.

25. Pandas are amazing tree-climbers and great swimmers.

26. Pandas mark territory by rubbing their scent glands (located under their tails) onto a tree.

27. A panda's superb sense of smell helps it find mating partners, and frequently allows it to avoid other pandas. A panda's sense of smell is so finely attuned that it can seek out the best bamboo even in the darkest dead of night.

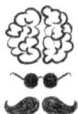

28. Pandas live up to 20 years. For captive pandas, life expectancy can even stretch to 30 years.

29. A panda's eyespots are initially round. With the time however they become increasingly teardrop-shaped. There is currently no scientific consensus on the purpose of these markings.

30. A panda's skin is black where its fur is black and pink where its fur is white.

31. Chinese philosophers linked the panda's black-and-white fur to the concept of Yin and Yang. Historically in China, waving a flag with a panda on it was used to stop a battle and to call for a truce.

32. A panda's skeleton is twice as heavy as that of other animals of a similar physical size.

33. An adult panda weighs up to 140 kg (300 pounds). Pandas grow so large that they do not have many natural enemies.

34. In 1963, the first panda was born in captivity.

35. As they poorly digest most of the food they eat, pandas produce up to 27 kg (60 pounds) of droppings every day.

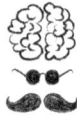

36. The panda is the most expensive animal to have in a zoo. They are five times more expensive to purchase than elephants.

37. A giant panda has always been the symbol of the World Wide Fund for Nature (WWF).

38. Pandas do not communicate using facial expressions.

39. A disastrous earthquake in 2008 in Sichuan Province, China, claimed many human and panda lives.

40. Some captive pandas would fake pregnancy in order to get attention and better treatment.

41. Giant pandas have 42 teeth and, like humans, two sets of teeth in a lifetime. They have the largest molar teeth of all carnivores (physiologically, giant pandas are carnivores, even though they prefer a vegetarian diet).

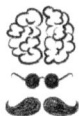

# Horses

1. Horses were domesticated over 5,000 years ago.

2. There are more than 300 breeds of horses.

3. Adult male horses generally have 4 more teeth than female horses.

4. Horses were only introduced in Australia in 1788.

5. Leonardo da Vinci enjoyed drawing horses.

6. A horse's brain weighs only half of a human's.

7. Horses cannot vomit.

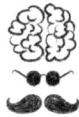

8. Like a fingerprint, zebras have unique stripes. By the way, zebras have denser stripes in warmer climates.

9. A horse's teeth never stop growing. Until it turns 9 years, you can easily determine a horse's age by just looking at its teeth.

10. Eating freshly cut grass can provoke colic in horses.

11. Horses use 16 muscles to move each ear. Usually, a horse's ear points exactly where its respective eye is looking.

12. A healthy horse's stomach should always make gurgling noises.

13. A red ribbon on a horse's tail usually means that it kicks.

14. Horses have seven blood types.

15. The underside of a horse's hoof is called 'frog'.

16. A horse's upper jaw is much bigger than its lower one.

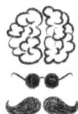

17. Aristotle was the first to describe the sequence of the horse's footfalls.

18. Horses have a third eyelid.

19. Horses do not focus their eyes like us. To see in the distance, they have to lift their head.

20. The horse in the Chinese zodiac symbolises intelligence and a free spirit.

21. Horses can sleep standing up.

22. Their gestation period is 11 months.

23. Baby horses can run a few hours after birth.

24. Domestic horses have a lifespan of around 24 years. The oldest horse on record lived for 62 years.

25. Donkeys live up to 40 years.

26. Ponies live twice as long as horses, up to 50 years.

27. On average, a horse's skeleton has 205 bones. Arabian horses however have one vertebrae and one rib less than the other breeds.

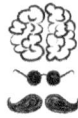

28. Horses have the biggest eyes among all land mammals, ten times bigger than our own.

29. Horses gallop at above 43 km/h (26 mph). The fastest recorded horse speed ever was 89 km/h (55 mph).

30. There are over 55 million horses in the world.

31. A male horse is a stallion, a female — a mare. A young male horse is a colt, a female — a filly.

32. The USA and the UK are the biggest horse meat exporters but it is only sold as pet food in their domestic markets.

33. Horses have no gallbladder.

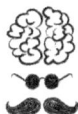

34. Stallions fight over females but do not defend territory.

35. All race horses have a common birthday: 1st January in the Northern Hemisphere and 1st August in the Southern.

36. Hippopotamus means 'river horse', though it is more closely related to pigs.

37. Horses normally do not laugh at you: they just try to smell you.

38. The name Philip means 'he who loves horses'.

39. A horse's official height is measured without its horse shoes.

40. The measurement 'hand' is equal to 10.2 cm (4 inches) and is still used to measure a horse's height. Anything below 1.48 m (14 hands 2 inches) height is classified a pony.

41. Horses are herbivores and have just one stomach (unlike ruminants which have four digestive chambers).

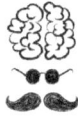

42. Horses produce 40 litres (11 gallons) of saliva a day. They drink at least 80 litres of water each day (20 gallons).

43. Horses can jump over 2.5 m (8 feet) vertically and almost 9 m (28 feet) horizontally.

44. A mule is a cross between a male donkey and a female horse. A hinny is a cross between a stallion and a female donkey. Mules and hinnies are usually sterile.

45. 'Zorse', 'hebra', 'zony' and 'zonky' are real names of crossed zebras with horses, ponies and donkeys.

46. Horses show their mood with their ears, eyes and nostrils.

47. Horses have an almost 360 degree field of vision with blind spots directly in front and behind them.

48. A horse's hooves grow at a speed of 6.3 mm (1/4 inch) per month. By the way, our hair and fingernails contain the same protein as horse hooves.

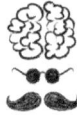

49. James Watt invented the term 'horsepower' as he wanted to measure the power of his steam engine and be understood. One horsepower = 746 watts; one metric horsepower = 736 watts.

50. On the Greek island Hydra, cars are prohibited and horses are widely used.

51. The Przewalski's horse is the only wild species. Mustangs are feral horses.

52. 'Chivalry' originates from the French word for horse: 'cheval'.

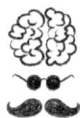

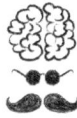

# Pigs

1.   In 2016, only one pig was living in Afghanistan, and more precisely at Kabul Zoo.

2.   Until the very end of the 20th century, the Bhutanese would feed their pigs cannabis.

3.   Pigs have 44 teeth.

4.   Pig skin is great for practicing tattoos, being similar to human skin.

5.   Pigs have four toes on each hoof, but use only half of them to walk.

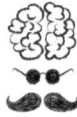

6.   The pig is part of the Chinese zodiac, and is believed to bring fortune and happiness.

7.   Not all pigs have curly tails.

8.   Pigs are clean. They never establish toilet areas close to where they lie and eat.

9.   Pigs have a remarkable sense of smell and are used to locate truffles.

10. There are many documented stories of pigs saving human lives.

11. There is a word to designate a litter of piglets — a farrow.

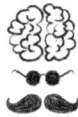

12. Piglets respond to their names at the age of 20 days.

13. Pigs were successfully used against war elephants. For example, the Ancient Romans lit pigs on fire and sent them squealing toward the enemy. A shrieking pig would freak out any elephant.

14. A sow's (female pig) pregnancy lasts 114 days. She typically gives birth to between 7 and 12 piglets, two times per year.

15. Pigs have a vast field of vision but cannot look up.

16. Pigs are quite intelligent and learn tricks faster than dogs. Their intelligence is inferior only to that of some apes, dolphins and elephants.

17. Pigs communicate with each other by grunting.

18. A piglet weighs about 1.5 kg (3 pounds) at birth and two times as much only a week later.

19. Pigs have no sweat glands and roll around in the mud to lower their body temperature.

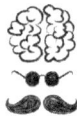

20. Pigs swim just fine and would actually prefer water to mud.

21. Pigs can run at top speed of almost 20 km/h (11.5 mph).

22. The words 'sucker', 'weaner', 'baconer', 'porker', 'chopper', 'sow', 'boar', 'piglet' and 'stag' all refer to pigs.

23. The words 'pig', 'hog' and 'swine' are used regardless of gender.

24. From a genetic point of view, pigs do not differ immensely from human beings. This makes possible the transplantation of pig heart valves to people.

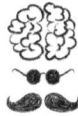

# AMAZING FACTS ABOUT YOUR BODY

## <u>Babies</u>

1. Between conception and birth, the weight of a baby multiplies by a factor of three billion.

2. An embryo's heart begins to beat 20 days after conception.

3. Unique fingerprints are developed three months after conception.

4. Every baby grows a fine moustache in the womb.

5. Babies are believed to start dreaming before birth.

6. Babies sometimes suck their thumb while in the womb.

7. In Finland, expecting moms receive a free 'starter box' of baby clothes, diapers and toys from the government.

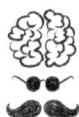

8. The inner ear is the only sense organ fully developed before birth.

9. Worldwide, five babies are born each second.

10. White babies, on average, spend five days longer inside their mothers' womb compared to black babies.

11. The tiniest baby ever to survive infancy weighed only 260 g (8.6 ounces) at birth.

12. The heaviest baby that survived infancy weighed 10 kg (22 pounds) at birth.

13. The term 'new-born' usually refers to a baby in the first 28 days of life.

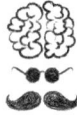

14. The word 'infant' derives from Latin, meaning 'unable to speak', and refers to babies from one to twelve months.

15. New-borns urinate on average 60 times a day.

16. Babies cannot shed a tear until they are approximately two months old.

17. Babies breathe up to three times as fast as adults.

18. In Europe, most babies are born blue-eyed.

19. One in every three babies has a birthmark. Girls are more likely to have one than boys.

20. New-borns are short-sighted and see only within a range of 20 - 30 cm (8 - 12 inches).

21. Babies double their weight during the first five months and triple their birth weight by the age of 13 months.

22. Babies in fact do have kneecaps. They are made of cartilage and therefore invisible to X-rays.

23. Babies are born with great swimming abilities.

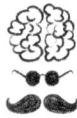

24. Most babies will lose the hair that they were born with by their fourth month of life.

25. A baby's brain contains about 100 billion neurones.

26. A new-born baby's heart beats on average 175 times per minute. For adults, this rate drops by half.

27. The mouth is the first body part to become sensitive to touch.

28. Babies can recognise their mothers by scent alone.

29. Babies love high-pitched singing, slow in tempo and with a lot of repetition.

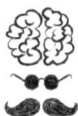

30. Premature babies (aka preemies) do not sweat during the first couple of months of their life.

31. One in eight babies is born prematurely. Famous preemies: Albert Einstein, Charles Darwin, Isaac Newton, Mark Twain, Jean-Jacques Rousseau, Pablo Picasso, Napoleon Bonaparte and Winston Churchill.

32. A baby's foot size at the age of one year roughly corresponds to half of their adult foot size.

33. A toddler's legs, pound for pound, are stronger than those of an ox.

34. A baby's head accounts for a quarter of its body length.

35. The brain of a new-born is roughly 10 percent of its entire body weight. In adults it accounts for only 2 percent.

36. Children slow down or entirely stop the process of growing while they have a common cold.

37. On average, babies born in May are about 200 g (almost half a pound) heavier at birth than those born in any other month.

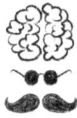

38. The largest number of children birthed by one woman is 69: i.e. 16 pairs of twins, seven sets of triplets and four sets of quadruplets. It happened between 1725 and 1765 in Russia.

39. Emilio Marcos Palma (born 7 January 1978) is the first documented person ever born on the continent of Antarctica.

40. Each baby shares his/her birthday with more than 20 million other people worldwide.

41. Reading to your kids at any age will expand their vocabulary, elevate their communication skills, and raise their knowledge.

42. Babies do not have bad breath as the bacteria that cause it live in tooth cavities.

43. Each baby develops a specific cry which its mother can easily recognise.

44. Most babies recognise their mother's voice at birth but it takes two weeks to learn their father's voice.

45. One in four children sleepwalks at least once before their twelfth birthday.

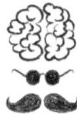

46. Children grow faster in spring but put on more weight in autumn.

47. Babies learn sign language long before they start talking.

48. On average, a woman needs over 2 minutes to change a baby. Rather surprisingly men do it 30 seconds faster, with an average time of roughly 1 minute 30 seconds.

49. A baby can read tone and will respond to it, rather than the words you say.

50. At the age of six months, babies can distinguish between individual monkey faces. A few months later, they lose this ability.

51. Babies laugh about five times as often as adults.

52. Babies can smile instinctively. They do not copy us as even blind babies can smile.

53. When a Navajo (Native American tribe) baby laughs for the first time, the whole family organises a party.

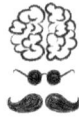

54. Unlike human babies, primates never smile at their parents.

55. One can distinguish French, German, and English babies just by the way they gurgle and cry.

56. By the age of three, children are aware of their gender and begin to act accordingly.

57. In 1909, a baby was given away at a lottery game at the Seattle World Fair, USA.

58. Babies love peek-a-boo as they lack the ability to understand that an object still exists even if they cannot see it.

59. In Japan, due to the ageing population, more adult diapers are sold than baby diapers.

60. Babies are considered self-aware when in front of a mirror they touch their own body and not the reflection. Psychologists think that a baby's self-awareness develops at around 12 months.

61. The number of sweat glands you have is directly linked to the temperature you experienced as a baby.

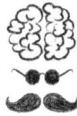

62. To have the look of a 'just birthed' baby in movies, they often cover a baby with jam.

63. Babies who are exclusively breastfed during the first three months have a 25 percent better cognitive development.

64. A new-born's hand grasp is so strong that it can support the entirety of the baby's weight.

65. The University of Montreal, Canada, published in 2013 a study stating that smelling a new-born baby can be addictive for women.

66. Babies sleep up to 17 hours a day. Unfortunately for parents, this sleep is irregular and tends not to last through the night.

67. White noise can soothe new-borns and help them sleep.

68. During their first month of life it may appear that babies smile, but they do not. The gummy grin is often because they feel gassy.

69. Babies cannot taste salt until the age of four months.

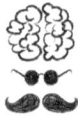

70. In medieval Europe, leeches were frequently used to treat most babies' illnesses.

71. According to studies, shaking the head to mean 'no' could have derived from babies turning their head away from food when they are full.

72. Caesarean babies are more likely to experience breathing difficulties.

73. 5 percent of new-born babies discharge milk from the nipples. Premature babies never have this condition.

74. Male babies are slightly heavier than female ones.

75. Scientists say that a baby's name influences their life as adults.

76. Babies can sleep with their eyes half-open.

77. Parts of a baby's skull overlap and leave the head temporarily cone-shaped after delivery. A protein called noggin prevents the parts of the skull from fusing together.

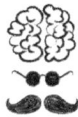

78. During pregnancy, the hormone relaxin extends the mother's ligaments a little, thereby permitting the bones of the pelvis to relax for the birth.

79. Honey can contain botulism spores; these release a toxin that can poison infants.

80. More and more babies are born on Mondays because doctors do not like scheduling Caesareans and induced labour on weekends.

81. Babies have many more taste buds than adults. Furthermore, these taste buds are not necessarily all located on the tongue: they can be also found on the tonsils and the back of the throat.

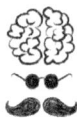

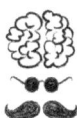

By Nayden Kostov

# Brain

1.   An adult brain weighs up to 1.5 kg (3 pounds), only about 2 percent of the overall body weight, but uses nearly 20 percent of the body's energy and 25 percent of the oxygen you breathe in.

2.   Your brain is about 80 percent water.

3.   The human brain grows the fastest between conception and the age of 5.

4.   You are born with all the neurons that you will ever have. They interconnect in the process of learning and their structure resembles the structure of the universe.

5.   Brain cells never regenerate. Once damaged, they cannot be repaired.

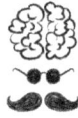

6.   Brain storage capacity is thought to be over 10 terabytes. That is many more times information than the entirety of the Encyclopaedia Britannica.

7.   The brain is split into two halves: each half controls the opposite side of the body.

8.   There are 12 nerves connected directly to the brain. They are responsible for the heart rate, most senses and facial movement.

9.   The brain contains billions of nerve cells that exchange signals with the rest of the body.

10. The brain works on electricity, transposed into commands to the muscles, thoughts and emotions. It uses roughly the same amount of power as a 10-watt light bulb.

11. No more than 16 percent of all electric connections in your brain can be active at the same time.

12. In order to raise your brain, eat more dark chocolate, fish, seeds and nuts.

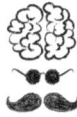

13. Humans possess a brain three times larger than those of animals of a similar body size.

14. When we touch something, the message goes to our brain at over 200 km/h (125 mph).

15. During the REM (Rapid Eye Movement) period of sleep, brain areas responsible for movements are shut down and our bodies are paralysed.

16. Your brain is more active and thinks more at night than during the day.

17. Scientists say people with a high IQ dream more.

18. The brain itself cannot feel pain.

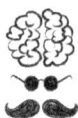

19. It is not possible to tickle yourself because your brain predicts the tickle.

20. When in love, the human brain releases the same cocktail of neurotransmitters and hormones that are activated by amphetamines.

21. You have many more than five senses.

22. You are able to see your nose at all times but your brain successfully ignores it!

23. The cerebrum, the cerebellum and the brain stem are the three parts forming the brain.

24. All thoughts, emotions and senses are processed in the cerebrum.

25. The cerebellum, or 'little brain', helps us keep balance and coordinate body movements.

26. The brain stem, connecting the brain to the spinal cord, controls important yet unconscious body functions such as heart beating and breathing.

27. The brain is actually floating in a fluid called cerebrospinal fluid.

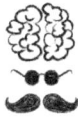

28. The brain controls body growth through hormones, produced in the pituitary gland.

29. Every memory you have is safely stored in a special area of the brain called the hippocampus.

30. Your brain normally shuts down if it experiences acceleration higher than 7G.

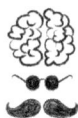

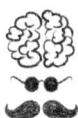

*By Nayden Kostov*

# Heart

1.   The heart beats 100,000 times a day and over two billion times in a lifetime. It would pump over 200 million litres (1 million barrels) of blood in a lifetime. This would suffice to fill 100 Olympic-size swimming pools or two oil super tankers!

2.   Squeezing a tennis ball really hard is roughly equal to the force used by our hearts to pump blood around the body.

3.   Four special valves in the human heart make sure the blood flows in the right direction.

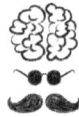

4.   The right side of the heart pumps blood up into the lungs and into the left side of the heart, which in turn pumps the blood out to the entire body.

5.   The human heart creates enough pressure to squirt blood over 9 m (30 feet).

6.   The heart rate is universally related to body size: the bigger the animal, the slower its heart beats. People have a normal pulse at 65-70 beats a minute. Quite slow, compared with hummingbirds and their pulse of 1250 a minute!

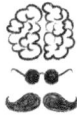

7. Women's hearts beat a bit faster than men's because on average women tend to weigh less and by consequence have less blood.

8. Each heart attack forms scar tissue, which does not contract in the same way a muscle does. These scar tissues can cause complications including heart failure.

9. According to a UK study, you are most likely to suffer from a heart attack on a Monday.

10. Contrary to the common belief, a defibrillator will not re-start a heart that has completely stopped beating. Rather its role is to fix an abnormal heart rhythm.

11. Electrocardiograph (ECG) was invented in 1902 by the Dutch physiologist Willem Einthoven. It is still used to observe heart rate and rhythm.

12. A spot in your heart, named the SA node, sends electric impulses to the rest of your heart, thus provoking contractions.

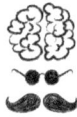

13. The only vein to transport oxygen-rich blood is the pulmonary vein (which connects the lungs to the heart). The only artery to transport oxygen-poor blood is the pulmonary artery (from heart to lungs).

14. The heart actually can keep beating after being removed from the body, provided it continues to receive oxygen.

*By Nayden Kostov*

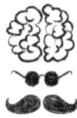

# Blood vessels

1. Veins, arteries and capillaries are the three types of blood vessels in the circulatory system. They transport blood containing oxygen, antibodies, nutrients, electrolytes and hormones. Blood vessels also transfer heat from the blood to body organs.

2. All blood vessels of a single human body have a combined length of close to 100,000 km (60,000 miles). Capillaries alone are responsible for 85 percent of this length.

3. On Earth, blood tends to pool in the legs because of gravity. In space, it stays in the chest and head. That is why astronauts have puffy faces.

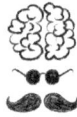

4.   The small arteries are called arterioles. They are less than half a millimetre in diameter, barely visible to the human eye.

5.   Microscopic veins are called venules. In diameter, they are below 50 µm (1/20 of the mm).

6.   Veins are not blue. They appear that way because only blue light penetrates skin and is reflected back into your eyes, thereby producing the illusion of blue veins. Blood in veins is dark red because it holds very little oxygen.

7.   Unlike most cells, red blood cells have no nuclei and thus are able to carry more oxygen. However, they cannot divide.

8.   Blood vessels' diameter is ranging from 25 mm (1 inch) in the aorta to only 6 µm in capillaries.

9.   A capillary's walls are only one cell thick.

10. Blood pressure is measured in arteries. The first (the higher) number is the systole phase or when your heart beats, while the second number corresponds to the diastole, when your heart is relaxed between beats.

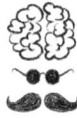

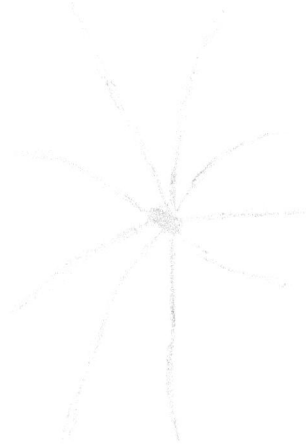

11. Capillaries are 10 times smaller than the diameter of a human hair. Red blood cells are pretty much the same size and have to travel in lines one-by-one. There are capillaries smaller in diameter than blood cells. They force the red blood cells to change shape in order to pass through.

12. The smallest capillaries are in the intestines and the brain. The largest: in bone marrow and the skin.

13. Veins hold up to 70 percent of the entire blood and are very distensible. They can endure huge changes in volume. Such changes may result from haemorrhages or blood transfusions.

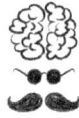

14. Blood samples are normally taken from veins, as they have thinner walls, larger diameters and lower blood pressure than arteries.

15. Larger veins possess one-way valves ensuring that blood travels in the correct direction and preventing the development of undue back pressure. Sometimes valves cease to function, causing veins to distend permanently, with blood flowing backwards and collecting in the vein. Swollen and enlarged veins are called varicose and usually have blue or dark purple colour. In appearance, they may be twisted, lumpy or bulging.

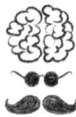

16. Varicose veins are a common condition, affecting up to 35 percent of adults.

17. The first recorded case of varicose veins dates back in 86 BC, when the Roman general Caius Marius described his suffering.

18. Giraffes have the greatest pressure in their legs amongst all animals. Yet, they never get varicose veins because of their extremely thick skin.

19. Being overweight puts extra pressure on your veins and valves, as they have to work harder to send the blood back to your heart. The impact of body weight on the development of varicose veins is thought to be more significant in women.

20. Wearing high heels for long periods can provoke or worsen varicose veins. As a preventative measure, keep your weight under control, exercise, eat a diet high in fibre and low in salt, and wear loose comfortable clothing when possible. Foods with high sugar or vitamin C can make varicose veins worse.

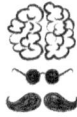

21. Any vein can become varicose, but as standing and walking put extra pressure on the lower body, they most frequently develop in the calves.

22. In 1929, the German physician, Werner Forssmann, invented the procedure called cardiac catheterization (a long thin tube is inserted in an artery or vein in your groin, neck or arm and threaded through to your heart). He first performed it on himself.

23. Most veins and arteries can dilate or constrict in response to nervous and chemical stimuli.

24. A vein specialist is called a phlebologist.

25. It takes about 20 seconds for a red blood cell to circulate around the whole body.

26. Blood plasma is up to 92 percent water.

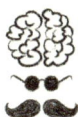

# Mouth

1. Teeth have their own nerves and blood supply.

2. The visible part of a tooth is known as a 'crown'.

3. A person can only taste food if it has been soaked in saliva.

4. Our tongue print is as unique as our finger and toe print and... our own smell.

5. A human tongue has anywhere from 3,000 to 10,000 taste buds. Pigs have almost 20,000.

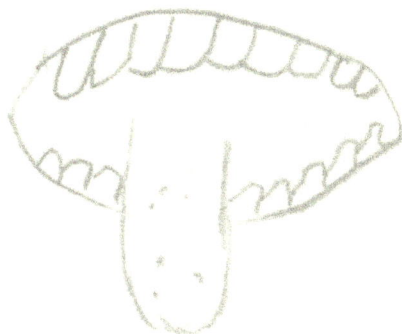

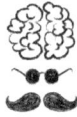

6.   The bacteria in your mouth are more numerous than the human population of North America.

7.   At the age of three one has 20 teeth. After losing them, an adult person grows 32 teeth at most. Some sharks however can have over 50,000 teeth over the course of their lives as they are constantly producing new teeth to replace the ones they lose.

8.   The mouth cools or heats food to the right temperature for consumption.

9.   Saliva starts the digestion and acts as a lubricant for your mouth. In a lifetime, you could fill two Olympic-size swimming pools with saliva simply by drooling.

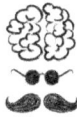

10. The tongue is the most powerful muscle compared to its size. It is also the only muscle not attached on both ends.

11. You always prefer to chew on the side of your stronger arm.

12. Humans have three pairs of salivary glands.

13. Lips tend to dry faster than the rest of the body because they have no sweat glands.

14. Lip skin has only three to five layers of cells. Lips get thinner with age due to the decreased production of collagen.

15. A sneeze speeds out of mouth at 170 km/h (105 mph); a cough — at 'only' 100 km/h (63 mph).

16. More than 10 percent of us grind our teeth while sleeping.

17. Food needs seven seconds to reach from the mouth to the stomach.

18. Teeth have four layers: root, pulp, dentin and enamel. Tooth enamel is the hardest matter in the body.

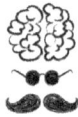

19. The vermilion border is where the lips meet the adjacent normal skin.

20. The name of the small thing dangling over the back of your tongue? An uvula.

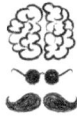

*By Nayden Kostov*

# Nose

1.   Your nose can detect dangerous smells in the air, like toxic chemicals.

2.   Even if you think you are a 'mouth-breather', you still mostly breathe through your nose. Your nose helps filter the air, removing dust and dirt from it, and also warms the air (or cools the air if it is really hot) to body temperature.

3.   Your nose has special receptors that are sensitive to odour molecules travelling through the air. These receptors are very tiny, and there are about 10 million of them in your nose! The brain, working with the nose, can recognize over 10,000 different smells!

4.   If you want to experiment with taste, get some of your favourite food and take a bite. Think about how that tastes. Then pinch your nose completely shut and take another bite. Notice a difference? Do you notice a difference when you have a cold? Most of your sense of taste is actually from smelling the food!

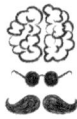

5. On average, men have larger noses than women. However, women are better smellers than men.

6. Mucous (or 'snot', as most people say) has lots of different jobs. It is part of what helps warm the air that comes into your nose, but it also adds water to it. That way, your lungs do not get dried out. The mucous also helps catch dirt and bacteria.

7. Did you know that you have no sense of smell when you are sleeping? This is why in case of fire for instance you would not be able to smell the smoke.

8. Dogs can smell thousands of times better than we do.

9. Your sense of smell is around 10,000 times more sensitive than your sense of taste.

10. Everyone has a unique odour, except for identical twins.

11. We grow over 2 m (6.5 feet) nasal hair in a lifetime.

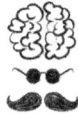

12. Olfaction is the term for the sense of smell. Hence the olfactory nerve, which enjoys a direct connection to the brain and activates memories when certain smells are detected.

13. Between your two nostrils there is a wall of very thin cartilage called the nasal septum.

14. A nose bleed can occur when blood vessels in the septum break. Many things can cause this, such as colds, dry air, exercise, allergies, bumping your nose, or (and I know you do not do this) picking your nose.

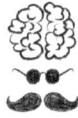

15. Behind your nose in the middle of your face is a space called the nasal cavity, which connects with the back of your throat. The nasal cavity is separated from your mouth by the tissue in the roof of your mouth, called the palate.

16. The indentation in the middle of the area between the nose and the upper lip has a name. It is called the philtrum.

17. Plastic surgery involving the nose is called rhinoplasty.

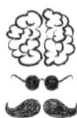

# Eyes

1.   We register over 90 percent of the incoming sensory information with our eyes.

2.   Eye lens act as filters for ultraviolet light. If they are surgically removed, the retina can detect UV rays.

3.   Reading in feeble light will not do any harm to your eyes.

4.   The more you talk, the more you blink. Women blink more often than men.

5.   We blink several million times a year. A blink lasts less than $1/10^{th}$ of a second and uses more than 200 muscles.

6.   Eyes can heal a corneal scratch in just two days.

7.   The cornea takes the oxygen needed from air, as it has no own blood supply.

8.   Tears first appear at the age of 1-2 months. The quantity of tears diminishes with age.

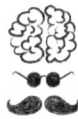

9. When crying, tears drain into the nasal passages and the nose gets runny.

10. Some 40 million people worldwide are blind.

11. Diabetes can cause blindness.

12. The biggest obstacle for a successful eyeball transplant is the complexity of the optic nerve. After the brain, our eyes are the most sophisticated human body part.

13. Rod-shaped cells in your eye detect shapes, while cone-shaped cells detect colour.

14. Each eye has a blind spot.

15. The muscles controlling your eyes are the most active ones in your body.

16. Dogs see colours differently than humans. They are unable to clearly distinguish between the colours green, red or yellow.

17. You read up to 25 percent slower from a computer screen than on paper.

18. The brain of the ostrich is smaller than each of its eyes.

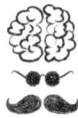

19. Colossal squids have eyeballs measuring almost 30 cm (1 foot) in diameter.

20. Eyelashes are renewed twice a year.

21. Normally, one of your eyes is stronger than the other.

22. Some people can see candle light from over 20 km (14.5 miles) away.

23. The Ancient Maya invested a lot of efforts to make their new-born babies cross-eyed. The Maya found slightly crossed eyes beautiful.

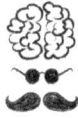

24. Men are more likely to suffer from colour blindness than women.

25. Only 15 percent of the human eyeball is exposed.

26. Your eyes have around 125 million light sensitive cells. The human eye still has better resolution than the best digital cameras on the market.

27. The iris is eight times more unique than a fingerprint.

28. Red-eye effect on pictures is caused by the capillaries in your eyes.

29. When sneezing, eyes involuntarily close.

30. If elderly people at one moment start reading without eyeglasses and feel that their eyesight improves, they should get their eyes checked as it could be a symptom of early stage cataracts.

31. A special enzyme in tears, lysozyme, is capable of destroying most bacteria.

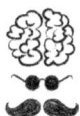

32. Your eyebrows are separated by what is called the glabella.

33. Eye colour, just as skin colour, depends on the amount of melanin. The most widely spread eye colour is brown.

34. People with heterochromia have two differently coloured eyes.

35. Wearing a necktie too tight doubles the risk of glaucoma. Glaucoma is an eye condition that damages the optic nerve, often caused by too high pressure in your eye.

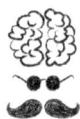

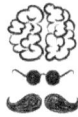

# Ears

1. The inner ear processes sounds and is responsible for balance. Tiny hair cells in the inner ear transpose sound waves into electrical signals which they send to brain.

2. Feeling dizzy after getting off an amusement ride? Blame the inertia of liquid in your inner ear's semi-circular canals.

3. Poking your ear with a cotton swab can actually rupture the ear drum.

4. We are born with approximately 3,500 sound-detecting inner ear cells. Sadly, they cannot regenerate.

5. Vertigo is caused by a dysfunction of the vestibular system.

6. Earwax protects ears from infections and cleans the dirt out. Production of earwax surges when one experiences fear.

7. An ear could get ripped off by a force of just 4.5 kg (10 pounds).

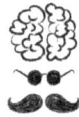

8. Ears keep growing throughout our lifetime. So does the nose.

9. Hearing quality drops after eating to excess.

10. Snakes have no eardrums and no visible ears, but they are not deaf. They have inner ear structures and are able to hear by feeling the vibrations.

11. You will find the smallest muscles at the same place where you find the smallest bones: in the middle ear. The middle ear bones got their Latin names for their shape — malleus (hammer), incus (anvil), and stapes (stirrup).

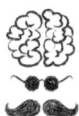

12. People with synaesthesia can literally 'hear' colours, due to overlapping senses.

13. Air pressure causes your ears to pop. Tiny tubes (the Eustachian tubes), linking the middle ear to the back of the nose, are tasked with equalising the pressure. They often get blocked when one has a runny nose, making flying on a plane painful or even dangerous.

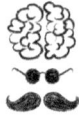

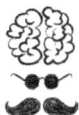

# Skin

1.   The skin, being the largest organ, stretches around 2 m² (20 sq. feet). It receives 13 percent of the overall blood supply.

2.   Unlike normal skin, scar tissue has no sweat glands and hair, and differs in colour from the surrounding skin.

3.   A plot of 6.5 cm² (1 square inch) of skin holds approximately 630 sweat glands. It also hosts on average 30 million bacteria.

4.   Each of us has more bacteria on the skin than there are people in the world.

5.   Callouses appear when one area of the skin is subjected to repeated or continuous pressure.

6.   Skin cells are born, die and reach the epidermis within less than one month.

7.   Each minute 41,000 dead skin cells leave your epidermis. This way your body loses up to 4.5 kg (10 pounds) annually! A great part of domestic dust is in fact dead skin.

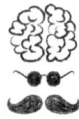

8. Lips are red because of the multitude of tiny capillaries contained within them which are full of oxygen-rich blood. Pale lips could indicate that the person is anaemic.

9. Some nerves are directly connected to muscles. In case of pain, they can command the muscles without involving your conscious mind.

10. The palms, the soles of the feet and the lips are the only areas of the skin without a hair follicle.

11. Depending on the hair colour, the average person has anywhere between 80,000 and 140,000 hair follicles on their head. Blondes have fewer follicles than people with darker hair colours.

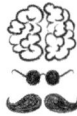

12. Goose bumps, goose pimples or goose flesh appear when one is cold or experiences a strong emotion (fear, pleasure etc.)

13. Skin grafts can be grown in a laboratory, multiplying by a factor of 10,000 from their initial size!

14. The three layers of skin top-down are the epidermis, the dermis and the so-called hypodermis or subcutaneous layers.

15. The epidermis, being the outer layer, is mainly formed of dead cells, from 0.1 to 1.6 mm (0.004-0.06 inches) thick.

16. The dermis hosts all sweat glands, along with the blood vessels and the nerves.

17. The hypodermis, being mostly fat, is great at absorbing shocks, and also hosts the hair follicles.

18. The more, the darker: this is how the pigment melanin determines the darkness of skin. Melanin also helps in protection from sun.

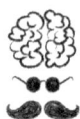

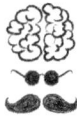

# Muscles

1.  Over 40 percent of our body weight is muscle.

2.  Muscles are great at pulling. However, they cannot push.

3.  Masseters are among the strongest muscles in body, helping us to chew.

4.  Bodybuilding will not help you grow new muscle fibres. It will only make existing fibres thicker.

5.  The combined strength of all muscles in the human body can theoretically lift 30 tons.

6.  There are 3 types of muscles — smooth, skeletal and cardiac.

7.  Skeletal aka striated muscles are consciously controlled. Smooth and cardiac muscles are not.

8.  You are probably right now sitting on your biggest muscle, the gluteus maximus.

9.  Smooth muscles make the food move through intestines and control the bladder.

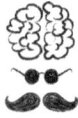

10. In absolute terms, a caterpillar has more muscles than the famous bodybuilder Arnold Schwarzenegger.

11. Idleness makes your muscle tissue disappear. Luckily, exercises can re-build it twice as fast.

12. Fingers are in fact moved from muscles in the palm and the forearm.

13. More than 100 muscles are directly or indirectly activated while you take a single step.

14. For each 0.45 kg (1 pound) of muscle gained, up to 10 km (7 miles) of new blood vessels appear. The same happens when you gain fat.

15. It takes more muscles to frown than it does to smile.

16. No animal has as many facial muscles as people do.

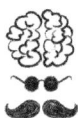

# Bones

1.  Cracking your knuckles will not increase the risk of arthritis. The sound you hear when you crack them is actually the sound of nitrogen gas bubbles bursting.

2.  Although bones appear very hard from the outside, inside they look spongy, filled with lots of air. Up to 50 percent of their mass is made up of water.

3.  The adult human skeleton has 206 bones. These are grown together from about 300 bones at birth!

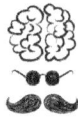

4.   The skull is made up of 22 different bones which grow together during childhood. It has only one moving part — the mandible (the lower jaw bone).

5.   Almost half of all bones in the human body are in the hands and feet, which allows for a great variety of movement.

6.   Bones in an adult account for 14 percent of the body's total weight.

7.   14 bones make up the human face.

8.   Bones are broken down and remade constantly, just like skin. All bone cells are replaced once every 7 years!

9.   Every second, your bone marrow produces two million red blood cells.

10. We are on average 1 cm (almost 0.5 inch) shorter in the evening than we are in the morning, due to the squeezing of the cartilage between our bones while standing and sitting.

11. The human body has 230 movable and semi-movable joints.

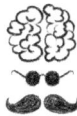

12. The hyoid bone, in your throat, is the only jointless bone in your body, i.e. it is not attached to another bone.

13. The longest and the hardest bone in the body is the thigh bone (femur), connecting the pelvis to the knee. Your femur is much stronger than concrete and as strong as granite.

14. The smallest bone is the stapes. It is located in the middle ear and only measures 0.25 cm (0.1 inches).

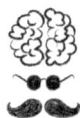

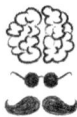

# Lungs

1.  The brain senses the amount of oxygen and carbon dioxide ($CO_2$) in the blood, and causes you to breathe faster or slower.

2.  Breathing only once per minute would provide all the oxygen needed. We need to breathe more often to get rid of the $CO_2$.

3.  The lung on the left side is smaller in size in order to make room for the heart.

4.  Babies are born with pink lungs that darken in colour as we breathe in polluted air. A person can expect to breathe in about 20 kg (45 pounds) of dust over lifetime.

5.  The lungs inhale over 2,000 m³ (70,000 cubic feet) of air each day.

6.  The diaphragm is a dome-shaped muscle below the lungs that makes breathing possible. Muscles attached to the ribs can also help with breathing, if the diaphragm gets tired.

7.  Ribs move with every breath, meaning that they move around 5 million times a year.

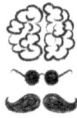

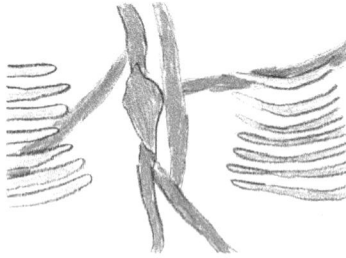

8. The lungs have 300,000 million capillaries, with a total length combined of 2,400 km (1,500 miles).

9. Special cells in the lungs produce mucous. They serve as the first line of defence against bacteria, dust and dirt entering your body.

10. It is impossible to commit suicide by holding your breath.

11. It is impossible to breathe and swallow simultaneously. Only new-born babies can do that for the first seven months of their life.

12. The larynx, aka the voice box, contains the vocal cords. These are two miniature ridges which open or close, allowing us to modulate our voice.

13. Combined, all 600 million alveoli (tiny air sacs of the lungs which allow for rapid gaseous exchange) have the surface of a tennis court.

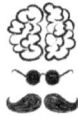

# Stomach

1.  You can survive without a stomach, a spleen, ¾ of the liver, 80 percent of the intestines, a kidney, a lung, and all the organs from the groin area.

2.  The stomach is generally the same size in most of us, contrary to common beliefs. It is actually located a bit higher in the body than most people think.

3.  When you blush, along with the face, your stomach blushes too.

4.  Burping releases the air you intake with food. In some cultures, it is a compliment to the chef.

5.  'Borborygmi' is the scientific term for the stomach rumble.

6.  The stomach can hold up to two litres (half a gallon) of food or drinks.

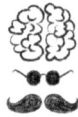

7.   In fact, digestion only starts in the stomach. The small intestines do the major part.

8.   Food leaves the stomach as a semi-fluid, called 'chyme'.

9.   Stomach acid (hydrochloric acid) can dissolve most metals and kills bacteria and viruses entering with the food. The enzyme protease, however, flourishes in such an environment.

10. The stomach resists hydrochloric acid only thanks to the constant renewal of its lining. When this process is not fast enough, ulcers appear.

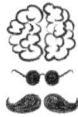

# Intestines

1.  We spend up to five years of our life eating. Over our lifetime, we eat over 7,500 times our own body weight in food (about 50 tons).

2.  The intestines' names reflect their width and not their length.

3.  At least 12 hours are needed to completely digest food. Food makes its way through the small intestine in about 2 to 3 hours.

4.  The small intestine is about 6 meters (17 feet) long.

5.  About 90 percent of what we eat is assimilated into the blood while passing through the small intestine.

6.  The effective internal surface of the small intestine is comparable to the size of a tennis court.

7.  The bacteria E. Coli, living in our intestines, help digest green vegetables and beans. It is also responsible for the production of certain, shall we say, 'gases'.

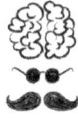

8.   On any given day we pass gas on average 15 times.

9.   Honey is easy to digest because it has already been pre-digested by a bee.

10. The appendix is in fact useful, accommodating bacteria that help the digestive system.

11. Smooth muscles in the intestines can move food even in defiance of gravity, allowing us to eat while upside down.

12. The large intestine mostly absorbs water. You can live without a large intestine; however you would suffer from permanent diarrhoea.

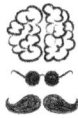

13. The nutrients from the food absorbed in the intestines are transported to the liver via the so-called 'portal vein'.

14. Most digestive enzymes in the small intestine are produced by the pancreas.

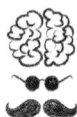

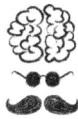

# Pancreas

1.  The word pancreas comes from Greek: 'pan' meaning 'all' and 'kreas' — meat.

2.  The pancreas controls blood sugars by producing the hormones insulin and glucagon.

3.  After each meal blood sugar levels surge and insulin is released to take care of the situation.

4.  When blood glucose levels get too low, glucagon makes the liver release sugars.

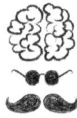

5. Beta cells in the pancreas release insulin. Their malfunction causes diabetes.

6. Known mostly for its insulin production, the pancreas also produces digestive enzymes.

7. The pancreas produces sodium bicarbonate (aka baking soda) in order to neutralise stomach acids in the intestines.

8. Pancreatic cancer is notorious for having the highest mortality rate of all cancers. It is hard to diagnose in its early stages, when a surgical intervention is still an option.

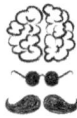

# Liver

1. There is a liver in every single species of vertebrate (animals with a backbone, or spinal column) so far discovered.

2. There are still no good means of artificially replacing the liver.

3. The liver filters our blood of chemicals which are then disposed of as bile. The bile then leaves our bodies as stool or is passed to our kidneys and filtered out into our urine. Bile gives our stool its characteristic brown colour.

4. The liver can regenerate after sustaining colossal damage. Liver transplants are possible — someone can donate half of their liver and the half that is taken will grow back!

5. Your liver also helps you when you have a cut. The liver makes the enzymes and other factors that your blood uses to clot.

6. The liver processes nearly all the medication you take.

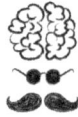

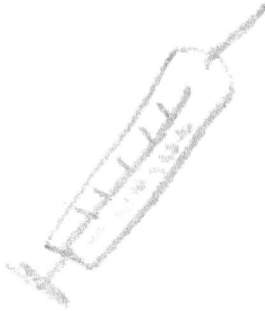

7. Scientists have counted over 500 different liver functions. Among the most important ones are: production of bile, plasma protein synthesis, red blood cells decomposition and detoxification.

8. Many things can harm your liver, including alcohol, viruses (hepatitis B), drugs and poisons.

9. A sign your liver is sick is if your eyes and skin turn yellow, due to unprocessed bilirubin. Sometimes the yellow pigmentation progresses so slowly that others notice it before the sick person does.

10. The liver transforms excess sugars in your blood and stores them in the form of glycogen.

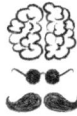

11. As glycogen absorbs water over six times its own weight, the liver plays a crucial role in water storage.

12. The liver also produces cholesterol — a key player in synthesising certain hormones and spawning new cells.

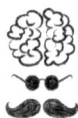

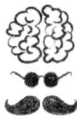

# Kidneys

1.   Inside each kidney there are around a million nephrons, acting as tiny filters of the blood. All the waste from your blood goes out into your urine.

2.   The kidneys keep the amount of body fluids constant. When dehydrated, kidneys will make less urine.

3.   If the kidneys detect a drop in blood pressure, they signal blood vessels to shrink.

4.   The kidneys cleanse about 1.3 litres (44 ounces) of blood every minute to produce about the same quantity of urine per day. The kidneys filter the blood approximately 400 times a day.

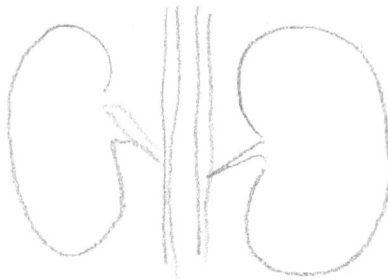

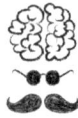

5.   Your body can work with only one kidney.

6.   Most donated kidneys usually come from a family member. A kidney transplant would be normally put in your pelvis and the disabled kidney will not be extracted.

7.   The yellow colour of urine is due to bilirubin.

8.   Your kidneys are responsible for activating vitamin D.

9.   The kidneys are connected to your bladder by tubes (ureters). When you pee, urine passes through the urethra.

10. When the bladder is about half full, your brain is aware that you need to pee.

11. The adrenal glands lie right above the kidneys and release stress hormones like cortisol and adrenaline. Adrenaline redirects blood to the muscles and prepares the body for the 'fight or flight' response. The adrenal glands change size throughout our lifetime. At birth, they are slightly smaller than kidneys, while adults' glands shrink to 3 mm (⅛ inch).

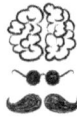

12. Should kidneys spot a drop in the blood oxygen level, they will boost the creation of new red blood cells by releasing a hormone called erythropoietin.

13. The Danish astronomer, Tycho Brahe, died of a ruptured bladder while holding his pee.

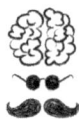

*By Nayden Kostov*

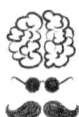

# VERIFICATION PROCESS

To start with, however a great read Wikipedia is, I have never used it to confirm facts; I rather checked the sources listed there and evaluated them.

Any fact has been confirmed by at least two (preferably three) separate scientific publications, be it on paper or online of the sort of http://www.science.gov, http://www.nasa.gov, http://www.sciencemag.org, https://www.genome.gov/education, http://www.howstuffworks.com, http://www.britannica.com, https://www.newscientist.com etc.

The scientific publications and websites of the best universities worldwide were also checked (an excerpt from the list): University of Cambridge, Stanford University, University of Oxford, Massachusetts Institute of Technology, Harvard University, Princeton University, Imperial College London, Yale University, Columbia University, University of Toronto, Humboldt University of Berlin, University of Tokyo, Heidelberg University, University of Melbourne, Peking University etc.

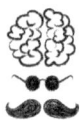

By Nayden Kostov

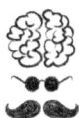

# ACKNOWLEDGEMENTS

This book is dedicated to my family: my loving wife Anna, my curious and restless sons Pavel and Nikolay, and my mother Maria, who sparked my interest in reading. Thank you all for being so patient with me during the lengthy process of writing. You are my inspiration!

Many thanks to the editors Jonathon Tabet and Andrea Leitenberger; to all test readers, friends, and colleagues who provided vital feedback and constructive criticism.

I am truly impressed by the Kickstarter community, which not only was great in the crowdfunding part, but also provided guidance and shared precious experience.

Zealous test readers:
Albena Vasileva
Alexandra Oliveira-Jones
Alexandre Berger
Desislava Morate
Laura Perkins

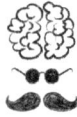

I hope you have enjoyed this book. I would greatly appreciate it if you would write your honest review on Amazon and/or on GoodReads.

You could also check out both my acclaimed trivia book **1123 Hard To Believe Facts** and my quiz book **Which Is NOT True? — The Quiz Book**.

Download a free sample from my website http://www.raiseyourbrain.com

There you could also subscribe for my newsletter and learn first about my next projects.

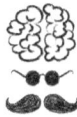

# ABOUT THE AUTHOR

Born in Bulgaria, I have lived in places like Germany, Belgium and Iraq, before settling down with my family in Luxembourg. With varied interests, I have always suffered from an insatiable appetite for facts stemming from an unrestrainable intellectual curiosity. It has certainly influenced my academic background and career: after acquiring Master degrees in Greek Philology, German and English Translation, I graduated in Crisis Management and Diplomacy and, most recently, undertook an MBA.

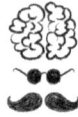

My career has been equally broad and diverse, swinging from that of an army paratrooper and a military intelligence analyst; through to that of a civil servant with the European Commission, and presently, that of a clerk, performing purely financial tasks in a major bank. Member of MENSA.

*By Nayden Kostov*

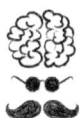

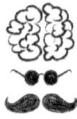

# FASCINATING FACTS FOR THE WHOLE FAMILY

*Author:*  Nayden Kostov

*Illustrations:*  Pavel Kostov

*Editors:*  Jonathon Tabet and
Andrea Leitenberger

*Format:* 5,25 x 8

ISBN-13: 978-99959-980-5-9
ISBN-10: 999599805X